Virago

Rebecca Ford

BookLeaf
Publishing

India | USA | UK

Presentation by *BookLeaf Publishing*

Web: www.bookleafpub.com

E-mail: info@bookleafpub.com

ISBN: 9789358312928

First edition 2023

*To those who understand, open your soul
and let go. You know how, even if you do
not remember.*

ACKNOWLEDGEMENT

To the love of my life, Daniel, as well as all my family and friends.
To the few who talk without words, thank you for your gifts!

Would you like to hear one of my horrible poems?

Longing for lost Love,
i'll Courageously throw my self over
the White Cliffs of Dover,
Wishing for the sweet
abyss of Death
like sweet plums of peace in the fridge.
Oh the Pain as the sidewalk ends!
Roses are Rouge,
Violets are Indigo,
When i write this poem,
how low can i go?
my Failure is like Finding
A louse on a bonnet,
or perhaps i should write
about the Road not taken and
do a study on Aging or Gender in a sonnet?
Woe to me, i regret
i have Traveled little,
remaining Geographically like Virgin
Mountains, Oceans, Lakes, Streams, or Brooks
full of Rain or Sunshine,
but i wish to make a poem,
Sing about the Cycle of Life,
sing of Beauty

as sweet as a Fiddle!
i write for the sake of
Desire in my Dreams,
to celebrate my Recovery and Friends.
i write to create like a
Mother Remembers giving Birth,
or a 5 star General conducts
a strategic War taking Communication
out first for a Win that goes down in History.
i write like i Thirst to Wed and
make Art of Milk in the Land of
Diet Coke.
i write through the grey haze and
cigar smoke.
As the seasons change and the sunsets
on the Poem from Earth and the
Moon rises as the God (or gods) of myth
dictate in a finite Universe of many
thanks to James Webb,
All before the Apocalypse and Afterlife,
i write till the Ink Well will
not "wrote,"
i Fear i'm Isolated and Ignamous for Eternity,
Alas this Poem is about sex, secrets and
Coming of Age in the Americas
as a poet.
i am defeated.

P.S. This poem is about all the themes of poetry
I could find on the internet and think of....

Forward and Back

I'm on my way Forward and Back
The Comeback-
The one I dream about
written in my future
(hopefully a long time from now today)
obituary.
I'm straightening shelves
for Habitat,
I've nursed my friends through surgeries,
painted the porch last summer (though it needs it
again)
Yoyo'd on and off meds
to see whats necessary.
It's been over 163 days
since I wanted an obituary tomorrow.
Forward and Back,
Forward to a future unknown,
Back to time cards, and paychecks.
Some people say there's nothing
wrong with you.....
That means my work is coming to fruition.
It means I'm high functioning
Both a blessing and a curse....
"With great power comes more responsibility!"
Thanks spider man and Darrin.

But the great power springs
Forward bubbling from a drowning stream of
weakness.
People do not see me when its 2 AM,
doing the dishes,
wondering if I'm actually
dead already deep in the bowels of
Purgatory of perhaps Hell.
He says, "I can't tell-your not acting like the
people in crisis I dealt with as an EMT."
I keep doing the dishes,
wondering if killing myself is the way into
heaven, and if he's a demon, or the Devil
himself.

But it's months later
And we talk in similar tones,
yet my brain is quietened by the medicines.
"I'm sorry for thinking
you were Satan."
He says, "No apology necessary-
It means you see me as a point of temptation."
I'm still doing the dishes,
Waiting for the water to trickle
down from the stream.
The dishes-always wet,
Waiting for them to dry
before I put them away in
my place in society again

Challenging myself to become
more than I ever have before.
I'm on my way back and now
Forward.

Kindred Soul

He with open eyes can see
What is there, the heart of me.
Three in the world have I found,
Who with me speak without a sound.
Eyes pass message, while mouths rest,
Chance encounters, with which I'm blessed.
Always when I'm at wits end
Mysterious angels with ears to lend.
They step and see with a second sight
Sending me on a revamped flight.
Somehow, I still seem to yet wonder,
How they pull me from from the under,
When I'm retching on my knees,
Cannot hear myself over my pleas,
That's when I look up and recognize,
An encouraging set of knowledgeable eyes.

Enlightenment

All alone, I can see the world pass,
At peace following my inner compass,
I'm led to the way I need to go,
I can see it all, so clear and slow.
I've seen heaven in the fading light,
Blind to others with hindered sight.
Ecstasy flying in the air,
Only I see it floating there,
The horizon glowing, causing my heart pain,
Breaking me like the sound of summer rain.
Soak it in, take in all of it's healing,
All those who see it;s new quiet revealing
In its solitude let your mind enroll,
In its azure skies, free your soul.

Hoping

I lie here and dream out the window,
Falling in love with one I do not know.
Who are you? Where are you now?
Will we recognize each other? How?
Will it be a smile or meeting of eyes?
On the first or numerous tries?
Maybe I will know when our fingers touch,
Or when we both laugh too much.
Are your dreaming of me too?
Looking for me, following ever clue?

Wolf

Here I am, a broken window on a stormy night,
With rain falling in and letting out the light.

Here I am, a silver wolf howling at the moon,
Singing my message of impending doom.

Here I am, a leaf in the winding wind,
Tossing and turning, searching for kin.

Here I am a falling drop of rain,
trailing like a tear wept in avoidable pain.

Here I am, a silk scarf tossed on the floor,
useless, abandoned, because it's carelessly tore.

Here I am, a sparkling blue bottle,
shimmering, beautiful glass, shattered once I
fell.

Here I am,
A scarf in the wolf's mouth,
the one living in a blue bottle,
watching a leaf blow south,
through a broken window,'
crying like the rain,

howling with the pain,
INSANE
my life like leaves in the wind
or shredded silk scarves.
I jump from my shelf,
azure glass every where
I sacrifice myself to the
wolf

Hide

I still remember,
The fires an ember,
Please do not try,
You know I will cry.
Just let it be,
Throw away the key.
I am hurting inside.
I am trying to hide.

Gone Bad

I left Animal Farm in the Free Library.
My gift to my intellectual child,
hopefully so they will surpass the peaceful life.
I used to be like Glaucon in The Republic, all
ruddy and exuberant,
yet my eros and thumos have fizzled out
and I due to bad advice in youth
sit quietly on the sidelines,
collecting banned books
from inappropriate Dr. Seuss pictures
to The Color Purple.
To be young and not limited in the race
To be able to be the Champion, only to be
assassinated in a theater or car,
loved in history for all eternity.
But that is not my fate.
I make a library that makes firefighters crave a
match,
Twisting ideas to inspire New Glaucons,
as I live as a socialist with my medicines held
hostage by the long race winners.
Yet who has really won?
For I am free to pursue the finer things in life,
love, cigars, mead, and thoughtful conversation.

Winds of Times

I stand in Forest Lawn Cemetery
watching the flags ripple and roll
in the winds intricate patterns.
-He was a hardworking man who lived simply.
He killed himself after a third failed marriage
but Uncle Menzo,
I will care for your grave with extra love.
You lost the battle, I now fight.
Death dancing and swirling
As flags in the cemetery,
Waltzing with me
When the medicines are not working.
You looked for a night on a couch-
so my couch is now open to a vet,
who is on a second failed relationship.
I too have couch surfed when relationships
failed
and have learned the lesson of a comfort couch.
I know it was not Grandma's fault, or even your
either,
but a genetic misfortune
in a time when torturous
Traverse City State Hospital was the only
option,
"couch surfing" yet to be.

How I have been blesses to
be in modern times with such a curse.
But I am well today,
as the winds of time dance through my genes,
a game of pre-life
Russian Roulette
in space and time.
So I care for your grave
with extra attention
feeling a bond as the wind
spins the pinwheel I place on it.

My Glasses

Please hold my hand in the dark of night,
where everyone is blind
and glasses, missed meds, and other medical
apparatus misplaced/misused
do not have power.
Sometimes when I can't sleep
I hold you like your holding me,
I'm still not sure how I lose my glasses,
but you have perfect vision in one eye so you
can help me find them.

A Love Poem

When I think about you
I am filled with angelic and animalistic visions.
Virtue and depravity (yet it feels wholesome
Overall reinstating my belief in the apocalypse.)
Everything about you engages my counterpart
      -your physical form
      -your intellect and wit
      -your heart and soul
We are like fire and ice on our top halves,
but centaurs on our bottom
creating steam ascending into the heavens,
while pounding the earth with our hooves.

The Game

The ordering of life's problems
Lining up to disappear
Invoking the idea that
IF I am just spry enough
with the controller
I can win eliminating disaster
IF only life was so simple
spin, twist, and place
Yet clutter does not disappear here
It compounds endlessly into the abyss

Shadows

In the shadows,
all things are on a sliding scale,
  my sexual attraction
  my gender
  my race
  my politics
  my health
  my life
even the little vacuoles in my cells point to the
reality that I'm partially dead.
So i make love,
checking boxes,
while eating and drinking,
running to feel and just breathe,
Stepping closer to the Son!

My Meaning

Learn to be
So we can be
with the I am
for eternity.
Learn to see
So we can see
with the Son
through infinity.
Learn the key
to be we
with the breath
in reality

Of Life

21

Learning to be with the still one,
whispering in the winds,
Learning to think,
with wisdom of pure love,
Learning we are all of dust,
and to dust we shall return
and then we KNOW.

The Dump Truck

 In college i had a friend who was my dump
truck and i was hers.
Now we each struggle along our separate hilly
paths,
Hers finished with a Doctorate,
dumping piles of papers into volumes of books,
my truck stalled at a bachelor's degree,
yet i am dumping papers with words at least
today,(though not nearly so many).
Today i saw a dump truck toy and thought of
her,
how we picked each other up into our mutual
activities,
with love and generosity, looking out for each
other for the good things
People still are dump-trucking me,
from one experience into another,
rubbing off my rough edges like stone in a
tumbler.
I hope as i grow older, i dump truck many to
their destinations,
knowingly and unknowingly,
paving roads, for dump trucks that will deliver
loads long after i am in the junk yard.

Hennessy

23

You give the feeling of safety,
Your brown and amber highlights,
with white foam on the ends,
Yet I do not drink,
I'm seeking to be your master,
while you strive to be mine.
It is bad enough I am slave to my cigars,
So I fight you to submission with a muzzle,
leash, and edible treats.
You pull and tug at the leash,
While I tremble and pull back.

You Have the Power

It is you illness,
It is your choice,
I will support you
how you want me to,
Your cross to bear,
Though I bare one too,
My boundaries of control
end in my finite body.
 I will be there for you,
through the bargaining, denial
anger, depression, and
finally the acceptance,
though it will keep cycling
as the illness progresses.
You may have to be there for me too.